21 Bebop Exercises

FOR VOCALISTS AND INSTRUMENTALISTS

PLAYBACK+
Speed • Pitch • Balance • Loop

To access audio visit:
www.halleonard.com/mylibrary

Enter Code
1647-7263-4404-3548

ISBN 978-0-634-03390-2

HAL•LEONARD®

Copyright © 2001 by HAL LEONARD LLC
International Copyright Secured   All Rights Reserved

No part of this publication may be reproduced in any form or by
any means without the prior written permission of the Publisher.

Visit Hal Leonard Online at
www.halleonard.com

Contact us:
Hal Leonard
7777 West Bluemound Road
Milwaukee, WI 53213
Email: info@halleonard.com

In Europe, contact:
Hal Leonard Europe Limited
42 Wigmore Street
Marylebone, London, W1U 2RN
Email: info@halleonardeurope.com

In Australia, contact:
Hal Leonard Australia Pty. Ltd.
4 Lentara Court
Cheltenham, Victoria, 3192 Australia
Email: info@halleonard.com.au

Dedicated to: my parents Gloria and Herbert, my sister Susan, my brother Jonathan, and my daughters, Marisa and Victoria.

Special thanks to: Larry Robison, Young-Min Koh, and Bill Green.

Audio mixed by Steve Deutsch at Mars Recording Santa Monica, CA

Photo by Maralee Frazier

Foreword/Introduction

21 Bebop Exercises was designed for both soloists and ensemble performers interested in further developing their proficiency with jazz interpretation.

As with many warm-up methods, this work concentrates on practice in all 12 keys. This will help develop dexterity and range, as well as instilling the benefits of each particular exercise.

By narrowing in on only 21 clearly defined examples, I believe you will find it easy to quickly memorize all of the exercises. Soon you'll grasp a greater understanding of chord alterations, phrasing, and note selection options available.

The most significant difference between jazz music and every other style, is the "swing" of the eighth notes. Although they are written as standard eighth notes, the true jazz feel lies about halfway between two even eighth notes and a dotted eighth note followed by a sixteenth.

Bebop originally derived its name from the fans and followers of jazz pioneers Charlie Parker and Dizzy Gillespie. Many of the phrases they played ended with two eighth notes sounding like the word "bebop."

Vocalists can use any sound. The most natural syllables begin with the letter "B" or "D" (e.g. ba, da, bee, dee, bow, dough). Also try sounds like "nah," "sha," or "sku." There is a universe of possibilities.

Most people choose to close themselves off in a room somewhere to practice while others are more motivated when they find an outdoor setting or mountain hideaway. The additional advantage of audio online enables you to download audio to play later or stream it now, anywhere you have an internet connection.

Many vocalists find warming up in their car on the way to a rehearsal or performance an ideal way to maximize the use of their time.
Please do drive carefully!

How to Practice with the Audio Online

Go to www.halleonard.com/mylibrary and enter the unique code found on page 1 of this book. All 21 exercises are recorded at moderate swing tempos. There are two hi-hat clicks (on beats one and two) followed by a bell tone (on beat three) which gives you the first note before every phrase. Some exercises start with pick-up notes.

B♭ instrumentalists: start on the third line (in the key of D); then jump up to the top to finish.

E♭ instrumentalists: start on the tenth line (in the key of A); then jump up to the top to finish. Change octaves as necessary.

Also to instrumentalists: I recommend that you listen to the audio and sing along with the examples. Then listen to the audio again and move the appropriate fingers on your instrument (without playing).

The **PLAYBACK+** audio player allows you to change keys, change tempo without affecting pitch, set loop points, and pan left or right.

Additional Practice Comments

Wind instrumentalists and vocalists, remember to keep the flow of air going when lines are going upwards AND downwards. Practice each line in one breath, then take another breath to begin each new line.

Range issues: Depending on your voice or instrument, some notes may be completely out of your range. These exercises will help you build possible range. Even "squeaking" out the new notes at first will help extend your range. When necessary, raise or lower an octave accordingly.

An additional note to instrumentalists: exercises that make substantial use of the fourth finger will naturally be more challenging than others. At first, concentrate on these at slower tempos.

The small box above each example contains the primary notes (in the key of C) that are featured in that exercise. Chord changes are included on all staves for additional comprehension.

Pianists have the option to play these exercises in unison with both hands in octaves.

One practice approach is to start from the last few notes of a phrase, then gradually add on more notes until the entire phrase becomes comfortable.

Another practice option is, after playing in all twelve keys going up as written, start at the bottom of the page, and work your way back to the top line of the page.

On any given day, you can choose to concentrate on only one, all, or any combination of exercises as part of your practice routine. Narrowing in on one at a time will enable you to build speed, confidence, and overall skill.

With regular practice, you will have these exercises to use as a framework when doing an improvised solo. At first, find places in your solos to quote some of these lines "note for note." Then try them in places where you don't think they'll fit. (Do they?) Gradually you'll find what you like best, then start altering the notes of these patterns as your ear guides you.

I also suggest that you transcribe and learn solos of your favorite soloists. Analyze the notes they're using as well as how they phrase and interpret them.

Finally, the more accomplished you become with these exercises, the more "chops" and knowledge you'll have at your command.

Remember, your goal is not to sound like Ella Fitzgerald or John Coltrane; rather, it is to learn as much as you can to best enable you to develop your own unique style and identity.

Thank you for the opportunity to share my musical ideas with you.

Enjoy!

Notice the tied 8th note pick-up. Relax, and "let it swing!"

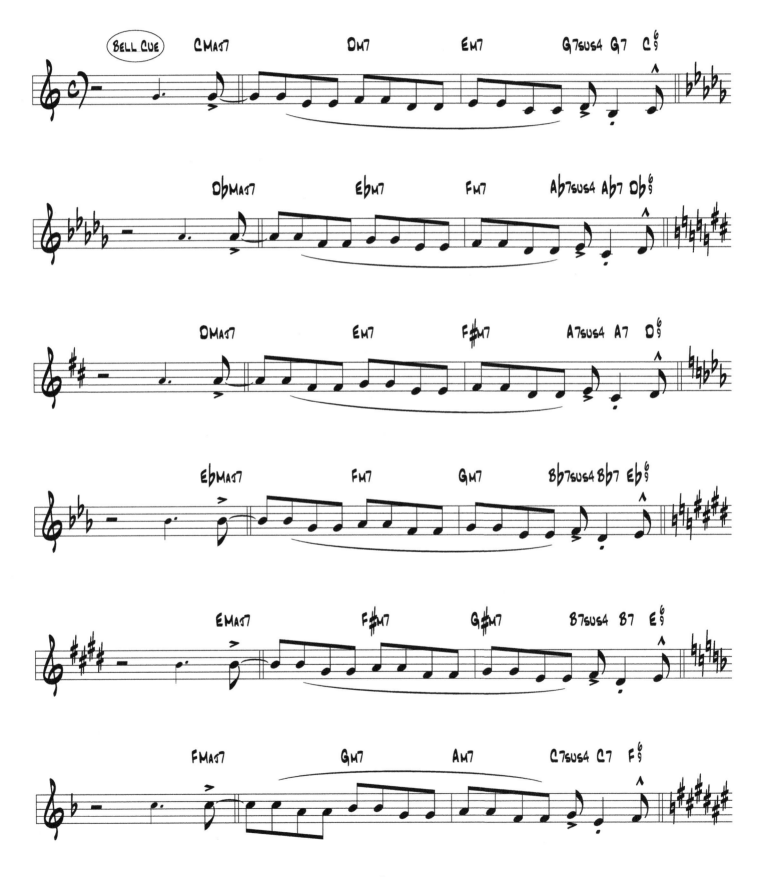

Acknowledge the accents and slurs. The sharp ninth is the same interval as a minor third.

Concentrate on accuracy and dexterity on chromatic notes within the distance of a perfect fifth.

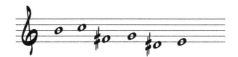

Familiarize yourself with this relationship - working with triads and their neighboring tones.

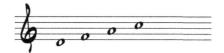

Up and down arpeggios of chromatic minor seven chords. Building this particular pattern up to your fastest possible speed will be invaluable to you.

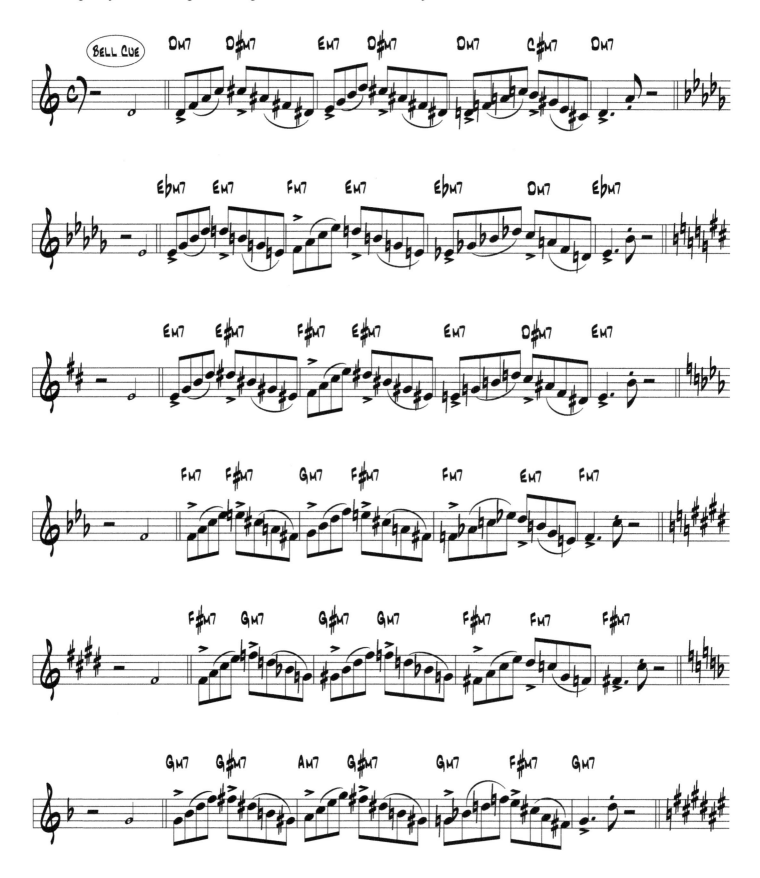

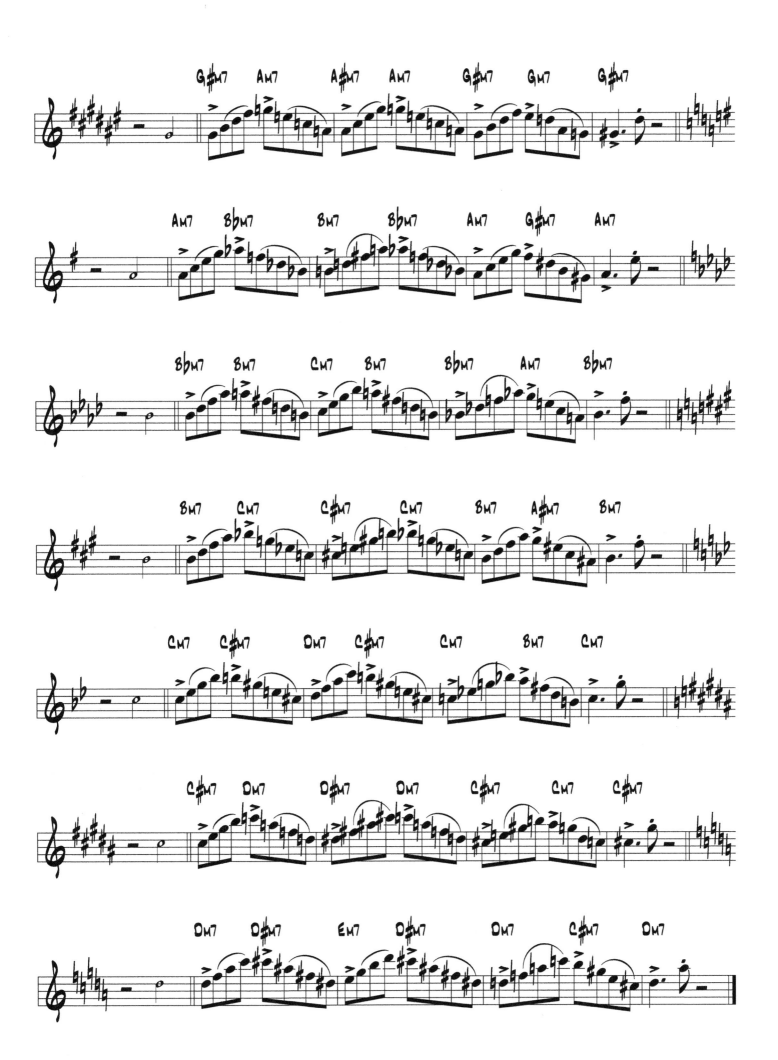

This pattern while in 4/4 time creates the illusion of being in 3/4.
(the box illustrates in 3/4 time)

7 - Focus: "Doubling Up"

When a tempo and your facility permit, the use of 16th notes can be very exciting and impressive. These notes swing in the same manner as 8th notes. (the box illustrates in cut time)

Descending pattern of II-V7-I chords through the circle of fifths.

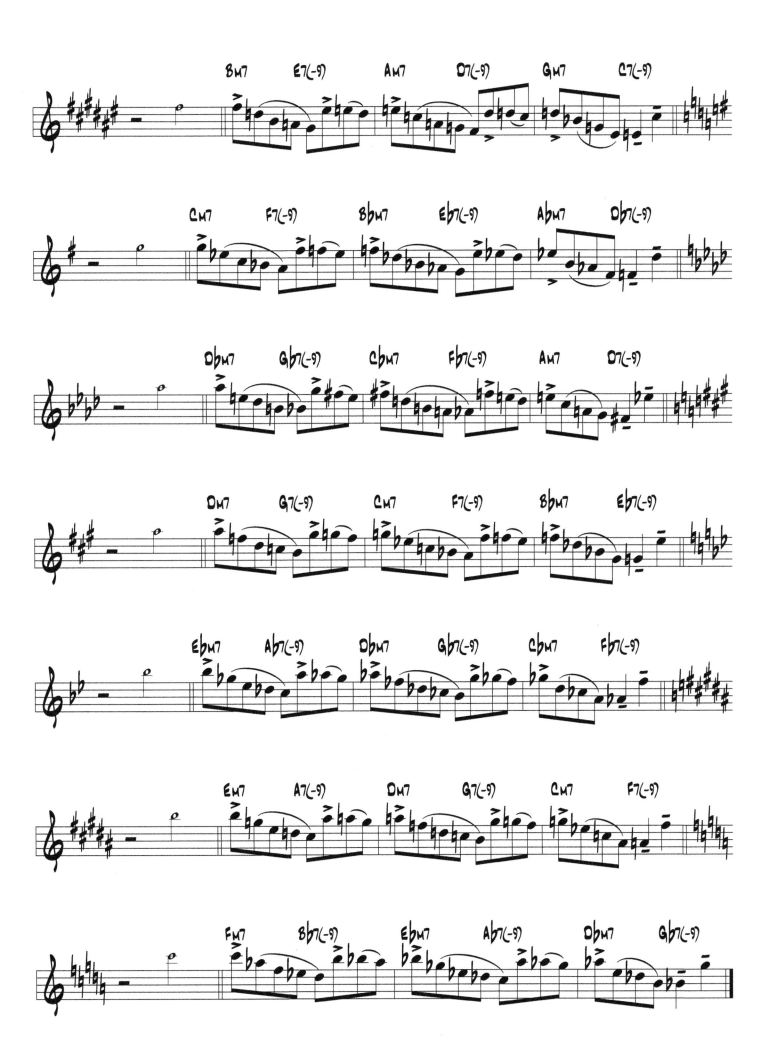

9 – Focus: Diminished Triads

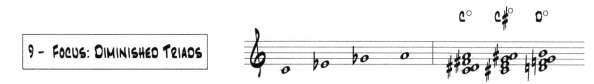

This pattern uses the each tone of a diminished chord as a new major triad.
Since Cdim, Ebdim, Gbdim and Adim all contain the same notes, there are only THREE possible diminished chords available. #2 - C# (E, G, A#) and #3 – D (F, G#, B).

Alternating notes between two different diminished chords can be referred to as a "Double Diminished" scale.

11 – FOCUS: FLAT NINE CHORDS

Notice how the four notes of a C diminished chord and a D7(-9) chord are identical.
(Other than the root - see box). Often diminished patterns work well with either type of chord.

12 – FOCUS: DIMINISHED PATTERN

A very "ear catching" pattern. Each note of diminished chord is followed by a tone raised by a half step, then a perfect fourth. This is the most challenging pattern in the book to execute, and well worth the effort!

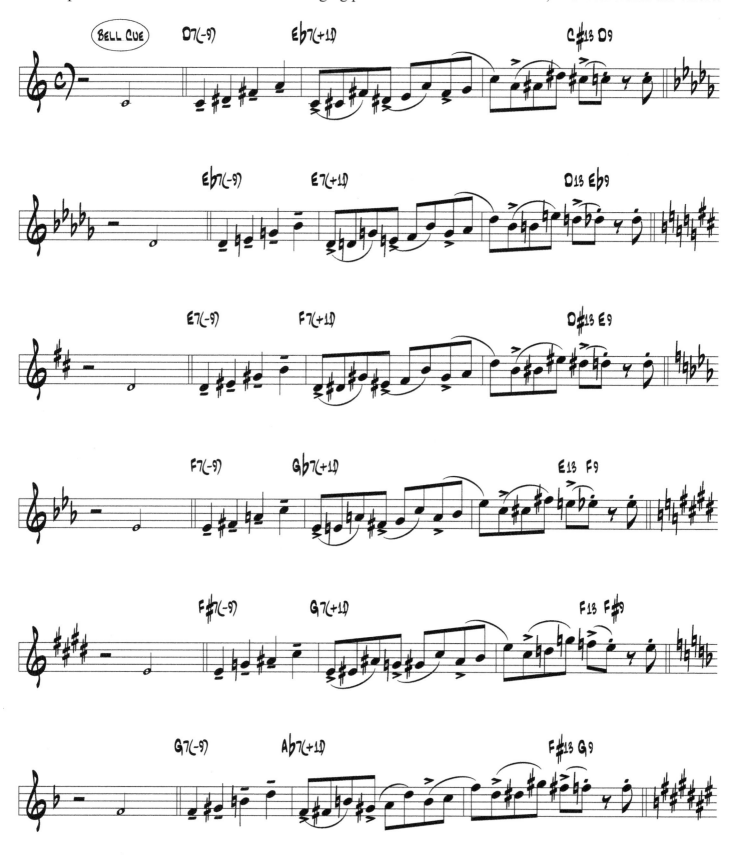

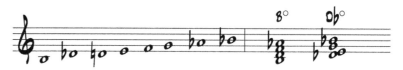

More practice with the "Double Diminished " scale.

Practice with minor I and IV chords. In a minor key, the V chord can be minor or major. Here's an example with both.

Often in a minor key, all of the IV chords will be major. Keep the arpeggios smooth and swinging.

16 – Focus: Blues Scale

The "Blues Scale" - perhaps the most fundamental notes in jazz.

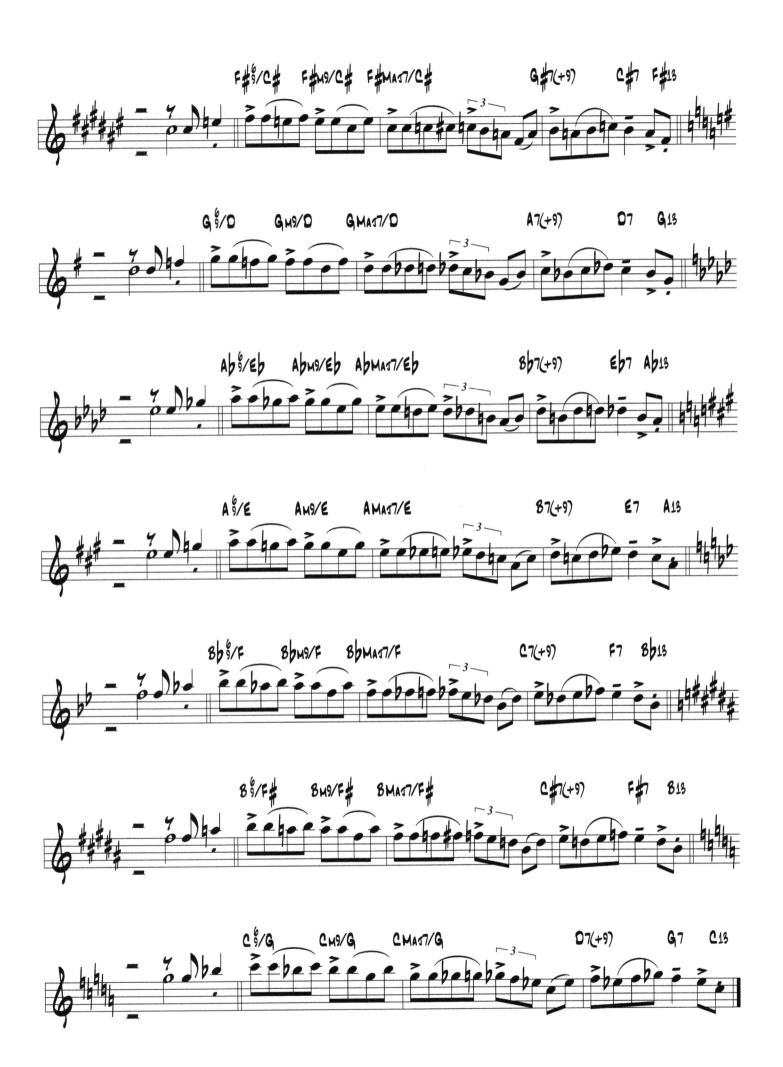

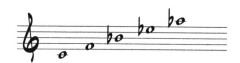

This pattern of perfect fourths was designed to increase flexibility and dexterity.

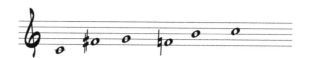

The "Flat Fifth" (or sharp eleventh) is sometimes considered the "most hip" of all note options.

All notes move from whole step to whole step in this scale. Perhaps most effective on a V7(+5) chord.

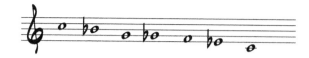

This pattern concentrates on long note to short note articulations based on "The Blues Scale."

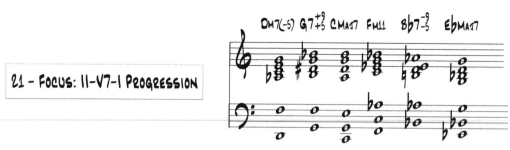

21 - Focus: II-V7-I Progression

Here we move from one II-V7-I chord progression to a II-V7-I up a minor third. An occasional trill can add additional interest.

JAZZ INSTRUCTION & IMPROVISATION

BOOKS FOR ALL INSTRUMENTS FROM HAL LEONARD

500 JAZZ LICKS
by Brent Vaartstra

This book aims to assist you on your journey to play jazz fluently. These short phrases and ideas we call "licks" will help you understand how to navigate the common chords and chord progressions you will encounter. Adding this vocabulary to your arsenal will send you down the right path and improve your jazz playing, regardless of your instrument.
00142384 ....$16.99

1001 JAZZ LICKS
by Jack Shneidman
Cherry Lane Music

This book presents 1,001 melodic gems played over dozens of the most important chord progressions heard in jazz. This is the ideal book for beginners seeking a well-organized, easy-to-follow encyclopedia of jazz vocabulary, as well as professionals who want to take their knowledge of the jazz language to new heights.
02500133 ....$14.99

THE BERKLEE BOOK OF JAZZ HARMONY
by Joe Mulholland & Tom Hojnacki

Learn jazz harmony, as taught at Berklee College of Music. This text provides a strong foundation in harmonic principles, supporting further study in jazz composition, arranging, and improvisation. It covers basic chord types and their tensions, with practical demonstrations of how they are used in characteristic jazz contexts and an accompanying recording that lets you hear how they can be applied.
00113755 Book/Online Audio.................$19.99

BUILDING A JAZZ VOCABULARY
By Mike Steinel

A valuable resource for learning the basics of jazz from Mike Steinel of the University of North Texas. It covers: the basics of jazz • how to build effective solos • a comprehensive practice routine • and a jazz vocabulary of the masters.
00849911 ....$19.99

COMPREHENSIVE TECHNIQUE FOR JAZZ MUSICIANS
2ND EDITION
by Bert Ligon
Houston Publishing

An incredible presentation of the most practical exercises an aspiring jazz student could want. All are logically interwoven with fine "real world" examples from jazz to classical. This book is an essential anthology of technical, compositional, and theoretical exercises, with lots of musical examples.
00030455 ....$34.99

EAR TRAINING
by Keith Wyatt,
Carl Schroeder and Joe Elliott
Musicians Institute Press

Covers: basic pitch matching • singing major and minor scales • identifying intervals • transcribing melodies and rhythm • identifying chords and progressions • seventh chords and the blues • modal interchange, chromaticism, modulation • and more.
00695198 Book/Online Audio.................$24.99

EXERCISES AND ETUDES FOR THE JAZZ INSTRUMENTALIST
by J.J. Johnson

Designed as study material and playable by any instrument, these pieces run the gamut of the jazz experience, featuring common and uncommon time signatures and keys, and styles from ballads to funk. They are progressively graded so that both beginners and professionals will be challenged by the demands of this wonderful music.
00842018 Bass Clef Edition $19.99
00842042 Treble Clef Edition $16.95

HOW TO PLAY FROM A REAL BOOK
by Robert Rawlins

Explore, understand, and perform the songs in real books with the techniques in this book. Learn how to analyze the form and harmonic structure, insert an introduction, interpret the melody, improvise on the chords, construct bass lines, voice the chords, add substitutions, and more. It addresses many aspects of solo and small band performance that can improve your own playing and your understanding of what others are doing around you.
00312097 ....$19.99

JAZZ DUETS
ETUDES FOR PHRASING AND ARTICULATION
by Richard Lowell
Berklee Press

With these 27 duets in jazz and jazz-influenced styles, you will learn how to improve your ear, sense of timing, phrasing, and your facility in bringing theoretical principles into musical expression. Covers: jazz staccato & legato • scales, modes & harmonies • phrasing within and between measures • swing feel • and more.
00302151 ....$14.99

JAZZ THEORY & WORKBOOK
by Lilian Dericq &
Étienne Guéreau

Designed for all instrumentalists, this book teaches how jazz standards are constructed. It is also a great resource for arrangers and composers seeking new writing tools. While some of the musical examples are pianistic, this book is not exclusively for keyboard players.
00159022 ....$19.99

JAZZ THEORY RESOURCES
by Bert Ligon
Houston Publishing, Inc.

This is a jazz theory text in two volumes. **Volume 1 includes**: review of basic theory • rhythm in jazz performance • triadic generalization • diatonic harmonic progressions and analysis • substitutions and turnarounds • and more. **Volume 2 includes**: modes and modal frameworks • quartal harmony • extended tertian structures and triadic superimposition • pentatonic applications • coloring "outside" the lines and beyond • and more.
00030458 Volume 1 ....$39.99
00030459 Volume 2 ....$32.99

JAZZOLOGY
THE ENCYCLOPEDIA OF JAZZ THEORY FOR ALL MUSICIANS
by Robert Rawlins and
Nor Eddine Bahha

This comprehensive resource covers a variety of jazz topics, for beginners and pros of any instrument. The book serves as an encyclopedia for reference, a thorough methodology for the student, and a workbook for the classroom.
00311167 ....$24.99

MODALOGY
SCALES, MODES & CHORDS: THE PRIMORDIAL BUILDING BLOCKS OF MUSIC
by Jeff Brent with Schell Barkley

Primarily a music theory reference, this book presents a unique perspective on the origins, interlocking aspects, and usage of the most common scales and modes in occidental music. Anyone wishing to seriously explore the realms of scales, modes, and their real-world functions will find the most important issues dealt with in meticulous detail within these pages.
00312274 ....$24.99

THE SOURCE
THE DICTIONARY OF CONTEMPORARY AND TRADITIONAL SCALES
by Steve Barta

This book serves as an informative guide for people who are looking for good, solid information regarding scales, chords, and how they work together. It provides right and left hand fingerings for scales, chords, and complete inversions. Includes over 20 different scales, each written in all 12 keys.
00240885 ....$19.99

www.halleonard.com

Prices, contents & availability
subject to change without notice.

0421
068